Text copyright © 2021 Marcus Amaker
Illustrations copyright © 2021 Nathan Durfee
Book design by Marcus Amaker

ISBN: 978-1-7374696-0-5
Library of Congress Control Number: 2021911485

Printed in the United States of America
First printing: 2021
*The art for this book was created digitally.*

Published by Free Verse Press
Free Verse, LLC
North Charleston, South Carolina
freeversepress.com

# BLACK MUSIC IS

WRITTEN BY
## Marcus Amaker

x

ILLUSTRATED BY
## Nathan Durfee

# BLACK MUSIC IS THE BLUES!

It's **BESSIE SMITH**,
the empress of analog emotion
and homegrown sound.
A renowned singer
whose voice was profound.

It's **BB KING** and his band
swinging with a personified guitar string,
and **LAZY LESTER**'s zydeco rhythm and blues swamp.
It's **BIG MAMA THORNTON**'s
"Hound Dog" voice divine
and rhythmic foot stomp ...

# BLACK MUSIC IS HIP-HOP!

It's the *Grind Date* breaks of DE LA SOUL
that take us *3 Feet High and Rising*.
It's mixtapes and soundscapes that are uncompromising.
The record-break spin of rhymes and a pen.
It's Southern lingo and trap. SABA, RAPSODY, and boom bap.
Beats, high hats, and hand claps.
It's streams of BLACK THOUGHT and bass-heavy flow ...

# BLACK MUSIC IS THE BANJO!

A lost history untold by radio.
Sold from West Africa
to the minstrel show.

It's **OUR NATIVE DAUGHTERS**
and the harmonizing of history.
It's listening to the voices that
don't get publicity,
like **GUS CANNON** and his band of jugs,
or the clawhammer roots
of **UNCLE JOHN SCRUGGS.**

The melodies were heard on many plantations.
It's **ELIZABETH COTTEN** - a folk sensation.
It's the fiddle, and covers of "Maple Leaf Rag,"
and **DOM FLEMONS,** who now holds the flag ...

# BLACK MUSIC IS JAZZ!

It's **ALICE COLTRANE** and her hands plucking sound.
**MAX ROACH** and his feet to the ground,
up and down between dust kick and snare.
It's **SHIRLEY SCOTT**'s hard bop
flow in the air.

It's **MAKAYA McCRAVEN** and **JEFF PARKER**
channelling the cadence of the Chicago sky.
Pushing the limit of improvisation
and playing notes on the fly.
It's **ESPERANZA SPALDING**
blending folk, rock, jazz and soul
because ...

# Black Music is Rock 'n' Roll!

It's **BIG JOANIE** and rrriot vibration.
The genius of **PRINCE &
THE NEW POWER GENERATION.**
It's **FISHBONE**'s feedback
in full **LIVING COLOUR**,
and **BETTY DAVIS**' funk
that sounds like no other.

It's the music of a people,
and the pulse of our heart.

It's a sound that was built by
**SISTER ROSETTA THARPE.**

# MARCUS AMAKER

Marcus Amaker is a poet, recording artist, and mentor. He is the author of eight books of poetry, including *The Birth of All Things* (Free Verse Press, 2020). The first Poet Laureate of Charleston, South Carolina, Amaker's poetry has been interpreted for ballet, jazz, modern dance, opera and theater, and has been recognized by the Kennedy Center, The Washington National Opera, The Portland Opera, Button Poetry, NPR, and others. He is the winner of a South Carolina Governor's Award, and is the award-winning graphic designer of the national music journal *No Depression*. He is a 2019-21 artist-in-residence of the Gaillard Center and the creator of the Free Verse poetry festival. In 2021, he received an Academy of American Poets Laureate Fellowship. He lives in North Charleston with his wife, daughter, and cat.

## MARCUSAMAKER.COM

# NATHAN DURFEE

Nathan Durfee has garnered notoriety across the Southeast for his captivating, pop-surrealist narratives and intriguing use of color. Currently based in Charleston, South Carolina, Durfee has been heralded as the Best Local Visual Artist by Charleston City Paper for four consecutive years, in addition to receiving the Teatrio Cultural Association book award for his children's book *Hello My Name is Bernard.* Each of Durfee's solo gallery exhibitions has been met with critical acclaim. Durfee has also recently been profiled in American Art Collector, Charleston Art and Charleston Scene magazines.

**NATHANDURFEE.COM**

# DEAR READERS,

I wrote this book as an opportunity for readers to learn about artists they might not know. And if you *do* know about these musicians, then it's my wish that BLACK MUSIC IS is a fun reminder about the power and depth of Black music.

I encourage you to purchase the music of each artist mentioned in this book. Spend time with each record, and also learn about the year that the recording was released. Social context is helpful when indulging in important musical works, especially from Black artists.

Our sound is the heartbeat and pulse of the world. It's nearly impossible to consume music in our society without hearing a note unsparked by a Black musician.

Why did I choose the specific bands and musicians in this book? Because I've always been in love with the idea of "deep cuts."

On his 2002 live album, *One Night Alone*, Prince said, "We are not interested in what you know, but what you are willing to learn."

That statement sums up everything about my relationship to art and music.

If I don't write about Motown, James Brown, Stevie Wonder, Nina Simone, Ray Charles, Whitney Houston, Aretha Franklin, Beyonce, NWA, or the countless other popular musicians - then someone else will. I love all of that music. And you do, too.

But from my earliest moments as a music consumer, I skipped past the "popular" section and went straight to the unknown. I loved underground music, flying under the radar of the charts.

That's why I want you to know about Elizabeth Cotten, Sister Rosetta Tharpe, Saba, and the others mentioned in BLACK MUSIC IS. These people are giants to me and deserve praise.

Praise YOU for purchasing this book. I hope you and your family enjoy it. It was a joy to write.

marcus AmAkER

# The Playlist!

freeversepress.com/blackmusicplaylist

SCAN ME

# The AudioBook!

FREEVERSEPRESS.COM/BLACKMUSICAUDIO

SCAN ME

# RECOMMENDED ALBUMS! *

Eddie Gale - *Ghetto Music*
Alice Coltrane - *Ptah, the El Daoud*
Moor Mother - *Analog Fluids of Sonic Black Holes*
Moses Sumney - *græ*
Prince - *LotusFlow3r*
Janet Jackson - *The Velvet Rope*
KMRU - *Peel*
Flying Lotus - *You're Dead*
Jeff Parker - *Suite for Max Brown*
Fishbone - *Truth and Soul*
Rapsody - *Laila's Wisdom*
Saba - *Care for Me*
Betty Davis - *They Say I'm Different*
De La Soul - *Buhloone Mindstate*
Esperanza Spalding - *12 Little Spells*
Our Native Daughters - *Songs of Our Native Daughters*
Big Mama Thornton - *Stronger Than Dirt*
Sly and the Family Stone - *There's a Riot Goin' On*

\* LISTEN ON VINYL FOR THE BEST EXPERIENCE

# BLACK MUSIC IS

www.ingramcontent.com/pod-product-compliance
Lightning Source LLC
Chambersburg PA
CBHW060944100426
42813CB00016B/2859